D0546776

Runaway
Duckling

You can read more stories about
the animals from Potter's Barn
by collecting the rest of the series.

For a complete list, look at
the back of the book.

Runaway Duckling

Francesca Simon

Illustrated by Emily Bolam

Orion
Children's Books

Runaway Duckling first appeared in *Moo Baa Baa Quack*,
first published in Great Britain in 1997
by Orion Children's Books
This edition first published in Great Britain in 2011
by Orion Children's Books
a division of the Orion Publishing Group Ltd
Orion House
5 Upper St Martin's Lane
London WC2H 9EA
An Hachette UK Company

1 3 5 7 9 10 8 6 4 2

A catalogue record for this book is available from the British Library.

ISBN 978 1 4440 0195 2

Printed in China

The Orion Publishing Group's policy is to use papers that are natural,
renewable and recyclable products made from wood grown in sustainable forests.
The logging and manufacturing processes are expected to conform
to the environmental regulations of the country of origin.

www.orionbooks.co.uk

For Jesse

Hello from everyone

Mother Duck

Quack
Quack

Five Ducklings

at Potter's Barn!

Mother Sheep

Baaaaa

Tilly and Tam
the lambs

Neigh

Trot the horse

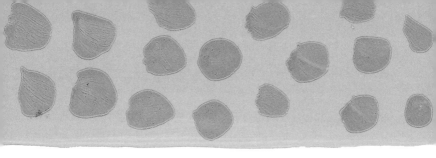

Father Goat

Bleat

Billy the Kid

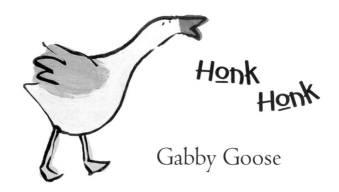

Honk
Honk

Gabby Goose

Woof

Buster the dog

MOOOO

Daffodil the cow

Rosie the calf

Oink oink

Belle the pig

Cock-a-doodle-doo!

Red Roost

Squeaky the cat

Miaow

Henny-Penny

Cluck
Cluck

The chicks

Cheep
Cheep

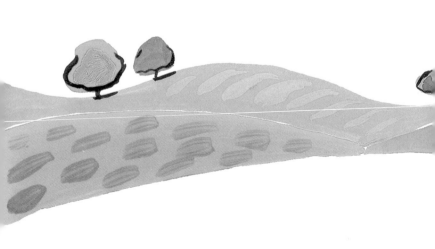

Welcome to Potter's Barn!

The sun always shines and the fun
never stops at Potter's Barn Farm.
Join the animals on their adventures
as they sing, stomp, make cakes,
get lost, run off, and go wild.

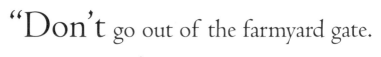

"Don't go out of the farmyard gate.
Don't go wandering in
Cross Patch Meadow.

Don't go to Far Away Field.
Don't go near Snapdragon Pond."

"And **don't** go in the old barn with the peeling pink front door," said Mother Duck.

"It's **dangerous.**"

"Yes, Mum,"
said the first duckling.

"Yes, Mum,"
said the second duckling.

"Yes, Mum,"
said the third duckling.

"Yes, Mum,"
said the fourth duckling.

But the fifth duckling
said nothing.

"Don't, don't, don't, don't, don't,"

she grumbled.

"Why shouldn't I go
and see all those places?

I'm **old** enough,

and I'm **big** enough."

While the other ducklings went
paddling with their mother
in Muddy Pond...

...the fifth duckling zipped
across Butterfly Field and
Silver Meadow towards
the farmyard gate.

Then she hopped through the
railings and waddled into the lane.

"Wow!"
said the duckling.

"It's great out here."

A milk lorry and a haycart swerved
to avoid the duckling as she stood
in the middle of the road.

BEEP! BEEP! BEEP!

"Cheep, cheep, cheep!" chirped
the duckling, waving to them.

Then she strolled along into
Cross-Patch Meadow.

She was too young to read
the sign saying:

DANGER!
RAGING
BULL!

"Isn't this a pretty meadow!"
said the duckling.
"And what a great place for a picnic.

Silly Mum telling me not to come here," she added, popping through the hedgerow into Far Away Field.

SNORT!

SNORT!

The duckling stopped to shake a pebble off her webbed foot, and didn't notice Samson the Tractor chugging along towards her.

Vroom
Vroom
Vroom
Phut!

"Hello, Samson," said
the duckling, looking up.
"What are you doing in the ditch?"

"Grrrr,"
said Samson.

"Nothing to worry about in Far Away Field," said the duckling. "What an old fusspot Mum is."

The duckling bounced happily
along to Snapdragon Pond.

"Great place to swim,"
said the duckling.

"So much nicer than Muddy Pond.
I'll jump in right now."

Splish-Splash
Splish
Splash
Plop!

"Lovely," said the duckling, shaking herself dry. "I'll tell everyone I've found a great swimming pool."

Then the runaway duckling
scampered across Windy Haugh to
the old barn, which stood alone and
dilapidated in Thistle Meadow.

"What a funny looking barn," said the duckling. "I must peep inside."

Creak
Creak
Cre-eeeak

squeaked the old barn door.

"Goodness, it's dark in here,"
said the duckling.

"Yoo hoo,
duckling,"
called a voice outside.

Who's that?
thought the duckling.

"Hello, duckling,"
said Buster the dog.
"You're far from home."

"Hello, Buster,"
said the duckling.
"I'm having an adventure."

"It's getting late now. Come on,
I'll give you a ride back to
Potter's Barn," said Buster.

"Great!"
said the duckling.

She felt like a queen as she
returned to the farmyard
on Buster's back.

"**Where** have you **been?**"
said Mother Duck.

"I've been so **worried.**"

"Everywhere,"
said the duckling.

"Cross-Patch Meadow,

 Far Away Field,

Snapdragon Pond

and

 the old barn."

"WHAT?"
said Mother Duck.

"And you know what, Mum?
No danger anywhere!"

Quack
follow me

Did you enjoy the
Runaway Duckling's story?
Can you remember the
things that happened?

Where does the duckling live?

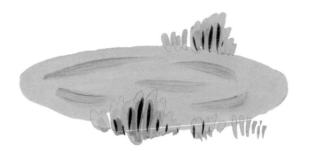

How many other ducklings are there?

Why does Mother Duck tell the
ducklings they mustn't visit all
those places?

What does it say
on the sign in
Cross-Patch
Meadow?

What's the name of the
tractor in the story?

What is hiding in
Snapdragon Pond?

Who else is in the barn
with the duckling?

Who finds the duckling
and takes her safely home?

For more farmyard fun with the
animals at Potter's Barn, look out
for the other books in the series.

Where Are My Lambs?

Billy The Kid Goes Wild

Barnyard
Hullabaloo

Mish Mash
Hash

Chicks Just
Want to
Have Fun

Moo Baa
Baa Quack